First Published in paperback by Laurie-Scott-Originals 2015

ISBN 978-0-9934043-0-6

Printed and bound by Laurie-Scott-Originals

Acknowledgements

I dedicate this book to all the children and the children within us all and of course, the cats who live on the streets and especially to the ones at the Cat-house community who inspired this book. Thanks also to Alex my two-feet Dad who encouraged us throughout the darker days and times of uncertainty. I want to express my gratitude to my lovely Grandma who gave my Mom the Walt Disney stories, and music and pictures in her childhood years, which helped her to grow up respecting all creatures great and small. I want to give a very special head butt and huge thanks to my Mom who translated this whole book for me, and created the wonderful pictures of family, my friends and me.

Prologue

This book was written by a cat called Shelley with help from her human Mom who translated it into human speak, and she created the illustrations. It is a story based mainly on true events, (no names have been changed). It is ideally suited for parents to enjoy while they read it to their children, (aged five to ninety five) and designed to amuse all ages in-between. It is especially appealing to animal lovers. Shelley's story is a humorous account of the well-travelled life of a street cat from Spain who now owns her own passport and personal suitcase, her transitions into her forever homes from wildcat to house cat; the adventures with her new family and friends found along the way. They say that cats have nine lives, and this book just covers two of them. Watch out for the next seven…

Contents

The Language of Cat

We cats do speak your language you know! If you use a little patience and take the time to observe us for long enough you will start to understand and communicate with us better. 'Cat' is our big name; just like 'Human' is yours. We have four feet and you only have two, so I think it is easier to refer to your kind as 'TWO FEET' Right···? Tell me, how does it feel trying to keep balance up there without two front legs, and no tail? I guess that is why you lot are so slow. Some stupid 'two-feet' are envious of our tails and some even believe that our tails exist just to make us pretty, but that is not so. My tail

is pretty of course, but sometimes a bit naughty too. It has a mind of its own, as it often tries to run away like a snake when I am cleaning it. That makes a funny game for me. Have you ever seen a cat playing catch with its tail? If you look closely, you will notice that we use our tails mostly for balance when we are running and jumping up high. We also use the movement of our tail to talk to each other. We do not actually speak with words and sounds like you two-feet do. We can if we want, but we do not need to. Our language is far more subtle than that, and does not always involve sounds; it is more like we think it in your direction. The only reason we choose to make the sounds is to make it simpler for your kind and to help you understand us better. You see, we cats are far more advanced than two-feet will ever be, and many of you don't really get it, do you? Did you know that? For instance, I am clever enough to be sending all this information to my two-feet Mom directly into her mind, so that she can make it into 'two-feet speak' just so that you may read it in what they call a book. This Book!!! There are only a few two-feet that understand the idea of our silent language; if they want to learn it, they will. On daily issues, we mainly communicate (Cat to Cat) with body language; it may be just a stare, the flick of a tail,

or a twitch of a nose or a soft touch from a paw. It can even be the angle that we point our ears, which can reveal so much. Have you ever noticed a cat staring into your eyes, and then she will slowly blink a few times? Each blink of those eyes is telling you how deeply she feels for you. That is the most powerful body language in the cat world. There are two main ways we tell each other things in cat language, as well as the mind talk, which is natural to all animals, except for birds, for instance when we see a bird that we want to make friends with, we normally make the "AKKA-KA-KA" sound. The aim is to make it sound as much like the noise that birds make to each other, in the hope that they will mistake us for one of their kind and let us get close. However, we are not the best at doing bird sounds, so you can guess the rest. It never works out, and they are always too fast at flying. They usually hear our bell before they see us too. Sometimes it happens and I get near to a bird, but very rarely. Now back to the important subject of 'think talk' or if you prefer you can call it 'mind talk'. A cat is able to make a thought extra strongly if she wants to let you know something important. Such as: "I want my dinner" or "I feel sad" or "I need to go out" or "let me in"

7

or "leave me alone I want my space", or most importantly "I need a treat"! There are so many important thoughts that a cat has daily, and it is YOUR job to understand and respond correctly to our thoughts. My name is Shelley and I have decided that my story shall be told, and I can; Because I am a cat, but before I do, I am going to introduce you to my fur family...

Me

Introducing My Fur Family

I met all my fur family before we took the big long trip to our new life in a place called ENG-land, and I know that it is a very long way from where we all were living before. Mom says that we four cats were born in Spain and that makes us Spanish, I guess that also makes us different, so we have learned to stick together. Let me introduce you to my fur family one by one in the order that we met, first up is Popcorn...

Popcorn Baby

I met **POPCORN** before any of the others came along. Our Mom also calls her by the second name of BABY; she calls me Baby too sometimes, so it gets quite confusing for the two of us. When Popcorn and I were first introduced to each other, my Mom told me that she was to be my new sister and I had been very excited, as I had lost touch with my real sisters a long time ago and missed them. However, sadly she was not like them at all! Popcorn was big and she growled at me a lot and was clearly not happy to have me as her

9

new sister. It was very unsettling for me as Mom separated us from each other at first. I remember being shut away in two rooms in the back of the house; although I did have a good view of the garden. I had lots of food and drink and had my own personal toilet. Mom used to come in and cuddle me for a while each night, as I would feel lonely and cry. I wanted her to be with me all the time. I could often hear her talking to Popcorn in the other part of the house and it made me sad. It took time, but eventually Popcorn calmed down, and I was allowed the free run of the whole place including that lovely garden, and Popcorn had to learn how to share it all with me. I think she has now got used to my smells and tolerates me quietly. Popcorn is a Tiger cat and she has stunning markings and of course, she knows it,

always washing that one, but now she is a little overweight. The fat one in our family; she takes after Mom I guess. Popcorn was Mom's first fur baby and I think she must have wrapped cotton wool all around her, as she is very soft. When I talk about our Mom, I mean our two-feet Mom, not cat Mom; all our fur Mom's have long gone over the Rainbow Bridge. I will tell you all about the Rainbow Bridge later... I think Mom is very close to Popcorn, as when we moved from Spain, I heard Mom all night explaining to her what was going to happen, and asking her to be strong for all of us. When it actually happened, Popcorn was very frightened and was unhappy to be leaving behind all her familiar hot smells. Popcorn's favourite trick is to hide. She likes to stay very still for a long time and then pounce out at us all when we have given up looking for her and are not expecting it. She is happiest when she is hiding inside a box or a cupboard or in a bush, but mostly you will find Popcorn high up in the outdoor world. I will never forget the first time when she saw two of her own face in that big round shiny thing that Mom calls a 'mirror'. Mom told her that it was just her 'reflection,' whatever that may be. I have not found any reflections yet, but Popcorn is quite fond of looking at her reflection and she can be found often staring at a mirror and pulling funny faces at it. In two-feet speak they call it being vain. Popcorn also enjoys long walks on the laptop keyboard belonging to Mom, especially when she is doing something important, just like right now as our Mom is making this story :-Q ·········Whoopee!!! She sometimes sneaks up to paw messages to Mom's two-feet friends, and it usually comes out something like this 'QWERTYUIOP', but it makes our Mom a little mad when she finds out. Another of Popcorn's tricks is to lap water directly from the tap; having learned that it made Mom smile when she was a baby. Mom and Dad said that it was delightful, so she decided to carry on with it. She is always watching the two-feet very closely trying to learn from them; sometimes she tries to open doors and windows with her paws when they are not watching her. It is just as well that her paws are too big and clumsy; otherwise, she would control the entire outside world.

11

Princess Purdy

The other one of our family is **PURDY**. Some say that she is a cat gone bad, but I don't agree. I met Purdy when Popcorn and I went to live with our Dad in Spain. She never came near me really, so that suited me fine at first. None of the others really liked her very much, but I started to get a bit closer to her when we first arrived at this ENG-land. That is when we were all so sad, and it was so cold. Therefore, Purdy and I cuddled up together to try and stay warm. Purdy is very dark, almost black in colour with gold shimmers when the light touches her fur. Purdy is skinny just like me. She is the oldest of us all, even though her passport says differently. I reckon Purdy is a very Spanish cat. I met a lot of her kind in the streets where I lived before. She is Dad's little Princess and thinks she can do anything she likes; there are often noisy confrontations between her and Popcorn, as they really hate each

other. Purdy is quite a solitary cat and only really appreciates the company of the two-feet. She will sit on any two-feet knee, even strangers, and apparently gets her name from the very loud PURRR noise she makes. I don't think it's as loud as my PURRR actually, but whatever…. Purdy really cannot tolerate many cats. No one knows where Purdy came from originally, even Dad. Apparently, she just turned up one day under a bush, as an older cat and that was it? We do not think that Purdy was ever a baby. Nobody knows her real age and she keeps this information to herself. She is very serious minded, and never laughs or plays with any of us cats. Some say that Purdy is a snob. She wears a crown, I am not sure why. She tells us that she descends from the finest of feline stock and that her blood is pure blue, like the sky. I have never actually seen her blood, but she tells us "one must believe" so we do.

Kitz - The Dog Cat

Kitz is a typical boy, the only boy amongst us. He likes to go out daily and catch treats for us girls. He also sees himself as our protector. I met Kitz when we moved to Dad's place and I actually quite like the boy. He told me all about his life and how he originally started living with a two-feet man who could not keep him, so he then moved in with another two-feet called 'Miss Lisa'. He was happy living with her, until everything changed when 'Banff' came along. At that time, Kitz's life was in real danger, so he was forced to leave and was sent to live with our Dad. Kitz really misses Miss Lisa like mad; he is always talking about her. When he found out that this Banff creature was a dog, Kitz decided he wanted to be a dog too in the hope that he could be with Miss Lisa again one day. He grew up quickly, thickened his tail, got brave and learnt to stand on his own four paws. When he heard them refer to him as "The Dude" on the street, he was pleased and became a real dog cat. Kitz works out, he is fit and he knows it. Kitz and Popcorn have become close friends since we have been in ENG-land· I think Popcorn is a replacement for his old Spanish friend 'George', who I will tell you all about later in this story·   Wherever we live, Kitz is always the one who escapes every day and does the boy things· They say he is the king of the street and has a reputation in the two-feet world as 'the dog cat'· He always comes back whenever Mom calls him, because he thinks that is how a dog would behave· I am not sure about that, because I have never been on speaking terms with any dog yet·   Kitz is the closest to that· Mom has just started this thing called 'jogging' and she goes to do it in the lane by us every day· Kitz actually goes with her most days and gets quite upset if he misses that 'jogging' thing· He prefers it when she does the 'Power Walking' as it is more like what dogs do· Kitz is pure white with a very soft pink nose, pink ears and pink paw pads· We do all rely on Kitz to guide us and show us the way, after all he is the only boy and he is the most daring & adventurous one amongst us· I guess you would call him pretty and really, he should be vain, but he is not· All except for Kitz, we three fur-faced girls started our lives as street cats·

My Story

Although I am the smallest, and I look a little fragile, my Mom says that I am the toughest of our family and I am the most streetwise. I lived outside on the street for many years so learned to look after myself.

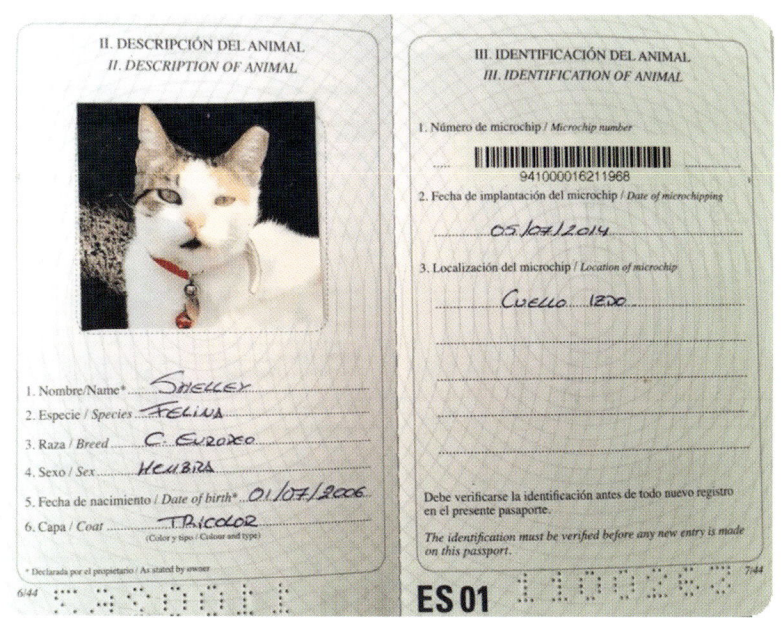

Mom calls me 'Shelley' for a name because of my colouring. She says I am like a seashell. I am what they call in Spain a Tri Colour; I know this because it says so on my passport. Tri means Three. My full name is 'SHELLEY BELLY WELLY BABY'. My colours are mainly White with Black and Orangey bits. I have always been proud of my coat; I do always try to keep my whites clean, and bright to keep my dignity, which was not an easy task when we lived out there in the muck and all sorts of weathers. Whenever they see me, the two-feet say my markings are unique, which sounds good. I have one big eye and one little eye and they say that you can tell from looking into my face that I have been through some rough times. Well yes I have!!! I do not trust any two-feet apart from my Mom. Many of the two-feet tell her that I must have been the runt of the litter; I am not sure what they mean by that, as although I am just small, I am also very strong and I know that I can survive anything. I do suffer with a small breathing problem; the vet told Mom that my heart is oversized and she took a picture of me inside to prove it, but Mom says that I have an extra big heart because I have so much love to give. I think Mom is right. I am so happy about the big heart my Mom gave to me since we first met, and she will always have my deepest feeling. It is wonderful to feel part of a real family at last, even though three of those are fur-faces; she my two-feet gave me all that! My main mission in life now is to keep my Mom's hand continuously stroking me as it makes me so happy. Sometimes I try to sit on her arm to stop her from moving away from me. She goes to a place called 'work' most days and it makes me very sad, as I miss her so much when she is not here with me. I wish I could go along with her! In the mornings we have a little ritual, I wake her up very early so that she has plenty of time to fuss me before she leaves for 'work'. I jump on the bed and give her loads of face kisses, head butts and rubs, as I am always very excited to welcome each new day and I feel that I need to tell her how wonderful it is to be alive, I am so very grateful to be here in this world with my family.

Popcorn   Purdy   Kitz

When I found Mom

We first met when I was living rough on the street. All we street cats used a broken old house for shelter. The two-feet call it "The Cat-House". It did not offer us much protection from the wet and cold, as it did not have a top cover on it as our house does now. I must explain at this point that I was not born with the name Shelley, my name before I met Mom was actually **'FEO'**; I only knew because that bad man shouted it at me all the time in bad language. In ENG-land speak; the meaning of **'FEO'** is actually **'UGLY'**. That two-feet made me terrified of others of his kind; MEN! I will not even let Dad touch me yet, because he also is a man. It takes a long time to learn trust when you have been hurt physically and mentally. (I found out that the bad man had a name too, it was Marco the Midget Monster). So, am I 'Shelley' or am I 'Ugly'? My mom says that Marco was very wrong to give me that name, and that I am far from ugly. In fact, I am beautiful. I do not really understand either of those words in either of the two-feet languages, because I am a cat, so I can't say. Only you can answer that question.

My Mom has made a picture of me to show you how beautiful I am. We cats can understand picture language too, so it is quite useful that our Mom is an artist and she makes many pictures all of the time. So what do you think, am I beautiful or am I ugly?

The Cat-house

We were 30 unwanted fur kids who squatted there at the Cat-house!

As I mentioned before, the wild time before I met Mom, was full of daily danger and there were so many of us living on the streets. The bad two-feet let go of their dogs when they were passing, they chased us and we had to run for our lives, it was very frightening. I think as a group they called us 'feral', whatever that means. I guess it is when you do not have any special two-feet bonds or a proper home. Our cat friends in the wild included 'Tiger' the local gossip who seemed to know everything, and 'Charlie Mozart' who was a big orange coloured tomcat. Charlie Mozart was very friendly and extremely vocal; that is how he got his name. Charlie had so many children, and they all loved him dearly. Then over

the other side of the Cat-house, you would often find 'Teddy Bear' and 'Tinker Bell' wandering around looking for food. They were sisters and whilst the Bear was pure black with very long hair, Tinker was so different; she was tiny and sweet with a pretty face, just like me. My Mom once tried to rescue her, but she did not want to leave her sister Teddy Bear. It was a shame that Teddy Bear's hair used to get very messy and our Mom used to go along and brush it for her, but it is difficult to keep your coat nice when you live out on the streets. Her hair was so long that Mom thought she was a boy at first. Another favourite friend was 'Poor Paw'. Our Mom named her thus because when she found her, she had just damaged one of her front paws very badly. I think she had caught it in a trap. Mom gave her medicine and tried to help her through the worst time, but it left her with a bad limp, and she was unable to hunt for food. Poor Paw's colouring was almost the same as Purdy's. In fact, she could have quite likely been her sister. There was also a cheeky boy called 'Oreo'. He had a very funny face and reminded Mom of a biscuit. We lived wild as a community and managed the best way we could. We looked out for one another. Sometimes bad two-feet used to come and take some of us away, so there was less in our community then. Because usually after they were taken, we never saw our fur friends ever again. It's just as well we knew how to make new ones, so as soon as they stole some away we made more fur babies to replace those we had lost. Not me though, I was clever and learned how to become invisible, as I did not want to bring any babies into this world of danger and uncertainty. We lived a tough life as it was either so hot that we could not find water, or there was too much water falling from the sky that we had to shelter from it so that we did not get swept along the street by it. At the times when the water used to fall from the sky, it had its benefits because we were left in peace from the bad two-feet, but sometimes it made too much wetness that it turned into rivers! I don't know if you are aware, but we cats don't like water at all. We cannot swim! So life can get a bit scary hairy for us. At those wet times, it was often difficult to find good shelter so many of us even used to climb up underneath those Metal Beasts and wait until the water stopped running, which Tiger says can be dangerous as you never can tell when a Beast may

20

wake up and start growling and moving fast taking you with them. I have heard horror stories that if you are not careful they will gobble up little cats into their big metal bellies. It used to give me nightmares!

The main problem was finding enough food to stay alive. Mealtimes were very rare, but sometimes kind two-feet used to throw stuff down for us, it could be such a challenge as we all used to fight over scraps and I am so tiny that I would more often lose to the others. I became quite solitary as a result, and would always hunt alone. I remember days on end that I did not eat and was often too weak to wake up,

a few of the others went over the Rainbow Bridge hoping to find scraps of food. We never saw them again!

On very rare occasions, two-feet took some of us away to give us nice homes, but they were only interested in taking in cute kittens and not fully-grown cats with dodgy looking eyes. When I was young I remember a time when a two-feet took me away from the Cat-house, but then she brought me straight back the next day. I was surprised to escape actually, and thought I was a goner. It was the most scared I had ever been in my whole life actually, even more than when the crazy man Marco wanted to kill me. That time is all a bit of a fur blur to me now, but whatever happened that day did hurt me quite bad and I noticed that my blood was red, and when I got back to the Cat-house it took me ages to come out of hiding. I stayed in the bushes for a long, long, time and I could not stop shaking from being so terrified! Then

21

the next day when I was having a wash I realized a strange thing, someone had bitten off the top part of my ear! That is what had caused the blood. To this day, I never found out why they wanted my ear, perhaps it was a tasty treat for some two-feet? Then I started to notice a few of my other fur friends had lost the top bit of one of their ears too. Two-feet are very strange. Mom says it is good thing they did that, as the ear biting may have saved my life, also it stopped me having kittens. I think kittens are furry babies. I wonder how any of this can be good, but it is all in the past now and I have to live with the fact that my ears, which some say are my best features, are ruined! Perhaps that is the reason Kitz prefers to play with Popcorn more often than me, I guess he must be an ears boy. **(Protection is given to community cats by trapping them and taking them to be spayed or neutered; and docking their ears to indicate that they have been neutered and then releasing them back into their community. It means we can live in harmony with our feral friends without losing control)** I think I would like to have kittens one day in the future now that my life is safe, but I am not exactly sure where to get them. Mom said we could find unwanted kittens at the rescue centre, wherever that may be. My dream is that one day she will take me there to choose some kittens of my

own. I don't even remember my fur-Mom and that makes me cry sometimes, but the others that had known her say that she was lovely, but not very strong and her main mission in life was making me born, so there you have it· Maybe the reason she went away and left me was to help me stand on my own four paws, also to help guide my two-feet Mom into my life? When I went back to see my family and old fur friends at the Cat-house one day I could not find anyone I recognised, just young strangers who chased me away· I did find that old scrawny Tiger cat with a loud voice that had always lived in the fields opposite the Cat-house; he was the local gossip and had some two-feet friends who looked out for him· He told me that the others had been 'culled' by some bad two-feet, and that our fur friends would be across the Rainbow Bridge by now· I do not know what culled means, but it sounds rather scary and most likely it was something to do with that evil Marco the Midget Monster, who lived near to the Cat-house· Maybe I had a lucky escape, however the Rainbow Bridge sounds quite nice· It is the place that they say we fur-faces go to when we leave this place and our soul leaves our body and floats away to meet a two-feet soul· We cats are always told this story by our elders when we are in our school days, and it gives us hope that there is at least one special good two-feet out there for each of us· It does often become a mission for many of our kind to find her···· Let me explain the story to you of the Rainbow Bridge and you can make up your own mind if it is true··· I guess you already know that there is a place called Heaven where all good cats and good two-feet go to find peace when their body gets too tired to carry on playing· There is a bridge that connects that Heaven place with where we are now· They say that this bridge is made of many different colours: Red and Yellow, and Pink and Green, Purple and Orange and Blue· None of my fur friends have actually seen it yet, but we are told that it shimmers with a light so strong that it is brighter than the sun and the moon· That bridge is just at this side of Heaven and on it, there is enough space for all of the good fur friends to live together, play, and be happy· At that place, our broken bodies get strong again, so I am hoping that if I ever reach it my breathing will get better· I hear that this is where all sick animals are fixed-up, as are sick two-feet; I guess it is a bit like going to a big vet in the sky. At the Rainbow Bridge, there is plenty of fresh food and drink and many comfortable warm places to sleep. (Sounds a bit like the rest au rant, which I will tell you about in the next chapter) That is where we stay and wait until our own special good two-feet comes along when their body is too tired to stay here as well. That is when they come and find us again, their own special fur child, then pick us up and cross the Rainbow Bridge with us and together we will run into Heaven, never to be separated again. So there it is, but really I think we should enjoy every day right now just in case all that rainbow story stuff does not happen and then we will have wasted time dreaming rather than living in the now time! It did initially make me a bit sad that I would never be able to hang out with any of the fur friends ever again, but in a way, that day was a real turning point for me. It made me realise that my past was truly past and I could bury it like a dog that buries their bone, and enjoy all the now bits properly, looking forwards as a very different cat indeed. Although I dream about it often, I never again visited the Cat-house after that sad day; in fact rarely did I even leave our outside space, as there was plenty of great stuff to smell and catch and my Mom was always near. So my peaceful days continued long, and warm, and the new family became more important to me day by day·····I reckon all of the good things that I have been told about that Rainbow Bridge are actually everything that I enjoy about today, and my future life with my new family.

Escape From the Cat-house

For us back then at the Cat-house it was hard to stay alive. Until this kind, two-feet started coming by bringing us real food. She used to come past the big wall every day and most of us came to rely on her. We recognised her sounds as she approached, and her smells were always friendly. Even the shyest cats popped their heads up from the bushes as she appeared. The rest of us would line up on top of the wall waiting for the food. She was very clever, as she knew if she put food down in one place, only the strongest bravest cats would eat, so she made sure all of us got plenty each and spaced it out all along the wall, so even little me got some! Sometimes we got real meat to eat and I started to feel less weak. We soon learnt that this particular two-foot would not hurt us like some of the other two-feet & we could learn to trust her, and I particularly enjoyed getting her on her own away from the rest of the gang and I would stare into her kind

face, and blink to let her know that I cared about her. She always made me feel less lonely. I really looked forward to those daily visits and it became the highlight of our days. I often used to dream that maybe she could be my own special two-feet. However, one terrible day she did not visit us, and we were all very miserable. Therefore, I decided to go and search for her. I found her at a place where the two-feet go to eat, they call it "the rest au rant" and I grew to learn that it was a great place for me to hang out too. I got so much good food and there was always plenty to drink, and the best part was that I did not have to fight off the other fur faces, so that become my secret place that I would visit regularly. (I truly thought I had gone over the Rainbow Bridge) There was another two-feet resting there that they called

"Chef" who gave me special treats too. There was stuff I had never tasted before that they called, "shrimps", "Chicken", and my favourites were "Steak" and "Salmon". Those were the good taste days. Often as I dozed in the sun under a bush feeling happy and full, my special two-feet used to come and find me, so I always followed her back to that heavenly place. The sounds that she made reassured me that I was safe. I spent more and more time at that rest place which I would have been more than happy to call my new home, if it were not for Marco the Midget Monster! He used to chase me away with a stick. He was the same man who had made me 'ugly' and I still do not understand what I did wrong to make him want to hurt me; but he did frighten me and the other cats a lot; he shouted at us, stole our drinking water away. He even made his dog chase us too. Most of the two-feet at that place were kind to me;

some of them wanted to touch me in a nice way, but I was still scared of them, so I would never let any of them get near. The only one I really wanted to be near me was that first two-feet that had saved me and gave me real hope. We became closer over time, I even let her touch me and it felt good. I was surprised. That was a first, as no two-feet ever had been near to me before that. She was my lovely two-feet Mom and I am so glad we found each other. At the rest au rant, my Mom used to run around a lot and I always watched her, but every day when the light disappeared, she would rest on what they call a step, and she would call me over to her by my new name of Shelley. (I guess that is how it got its name rest au rant, and the 'rant' bit must have come from Marco the Midget Monster!) That step is the exact spot where I got my brave tail and let it touch my Mom for the first time proper. Then, every day after that was better and better and better. It just felt too nice when my little tail made contact with her, and from that day onward, it was the most important place for me to be in the whole world. My 'real' life as Shelley had just begun.

Goodbye Street Life

That evil man Marco with the hurt stick seemed to want to ruin it all for us. He used to rant and rave and wave his stick every day, and he was always arguing loudly with my newfound family at the rest au rant. He was mostly going on about his father's friend "Franco" and how much better things were when he had been in charge. I am not sure what he meant, as for me, life was better than ever···, but Mom told me that he was a bit crazy and we needed to keep away from him. That was difficult, as he would sometimes creep up when I was asleep under the hedge and jab at me with his stick. Good overcame evil in the end and we all escaped from him. My parents did not like Marco either, so the outcome was saying goodbye to that lovely place where we all rested. The three of us left together Mom, Dad and me. This made us all a bit sad, but none of us wanted the constant harassing that we got every single day from that evil two-feet man. I do not know why he was so powerful and evil. I remember one night just before it all ended, when my new two-feet Dad (Mom's best friend) brought me inside the rest au rant, locked the door and stayed with me all night to protect me from that bad Monster man who wanted to kill me. I do not know why he wanted to do that; but it was a strange and scary time for us all. The next day my Mom took me far away from all that danger. I remember the day so well; I was terrified, as I did not know what was happening. I squeezed into a tiny box inside a big Metal Beast which took us to the new indoor house with a top to shelter under, and that is exactly the time when I first met Popcorn my new fur sister. As I mentioned before, she did not like me from the first day, and I was unsure of how to make friends with her, so we were kept separate for a while. Now looking back, I think Popcorn was confused, as it had always been just her and Mom before I came along and she had all of the attention, so understandably she felt angry when she had to share everything with me so suddenly. Back then, I was oh

28

so confused and I think Popcorn must have been as well. We now tolerate each other because we are both Mom's little girls and we want Mom to be happy. That time is a bit of a fur blur to me now, but a very happy blur where I grew into my first proper family and said goodbye to my wild life, and that evil crazy man; I never saw him ever again. From then onwards, I had two regular meals everyday and I could drink

whenever I wanted, also we had extra little things called "treats" which were amazing! The first time I got one I did not know whether to fight it, lick it, or play with it, but I eventually got the right idea. It was for me to eat; the most amazing taste exploded into my mouth. Delicious! Mom always tells us that treats are for good cats only, so I try always to be good. I had a real comfortable warm place to sleep, which they called a bed, and for the first time in my life, I felt very safe. In the daytime, I was allowed to go out, play, and catch Lizards or anything else that I wanted. We three lived as a real family, Shelley, Popcorn and Mom, and I was the happiest cat in Spain!

Mom and Dad Wanted to Be Together

Everything was to change when Mom wanted to be with Dad. They took both Popcorn and me to a new bigger place with lots of steps separating an up and down section; it also had a huge lid to keep the cold and wet out. To begin with, Mom lived in the lower part with us, which was fine, but I was curious to meet the others as I had already picked up their smells and so it did not take long before we joined up with Kitz and Purdy who lived upstairs with Dad and we all started living together. So then there were four of us fur babies. We did not get along too well at first, but soon got used to each other and we learned to give each of us our own space. Space is so important to us cats, and we really need to have our own good smells around to be able to relax completely. Two-feet call it our territory and they laugh at us, but they are quite similar to us in some ways, as they like their own space too. They get their smells in bottles but our smells are built into us already. Have you ever noticed us rolling around and rubbing against things with our faces? That is when we are marking our good smell boundary, it is a bit like drawing a circle around where we live and protecting it, we then know immediately if a strange smell enters that circle. We will chase it away to keep all the smells right and orderly. It takes a long time for us cats to make a family and get used to each other's smells, but when we do, it is forever. We had a great life at that place because Dad used to leave a door open for us all so that we could come and go as we wanted. I never wanted to go too far away, as I had lived wild on the streets all of my life before, and was beginning to appreciate the comfort and safety of an inside life. By the way, the two-feet call that lid on top of a house a 'roof' and it is such a great idea as it keeps us all so dry. Popcorn caused many problems for our two-feet at that time, as she did not like the new smells at Dad's place and was running away every day. She kept going back to our old place where she could find her happy smells, that is where she had lived with just Mom. Except for Purdy, we were all quite worried about her, as she was so miserable and many nights she would escape. We would hear our parents walking around the area outside calling "Baby", and she would run and hide from them on purpose. Poor Popcorn was really quite fed-up about having to share her life with three other fur-faces. She had always been the only fur child in her own territory and as she had found our Mom when she was a kitten, she thought she should be the only one. After all the running away, Mom chose to keep the door closed for a while to stop her escaping and she was very unhappy about that. I did not mind, although I remember hearing her pawing the floor for ages and it sounded like she was trying to open the door. She was so angry about being a prisoner. She scratched, wailed, and caused a big stir. Popcorn eventually calmed down, and became used to the new smells and she stopped running away. Purdy always made her life miserable though. I guess you can understand that a bit, because it had been Purdy's home with Kitz and Dad. We were the intruders with all our strange smells, just like when I first arrived into Popcorn's life with Mom before. It all goes around and around and we all learn lots of lessons in getting along and understanding each other's ways and living in harmony together…

George

It was at Dad's place in Spain when Kitz our brother really started to find friends.... We suddenly started getting a new boy smell into our circle, and that smell was from 'GEORGE'. Whenever he appeared, Kitz always closely followed him. George and Kitz became inseparable and none of us dared chase him away. He was what two-feet call an Alpha Cat. George was a street chap, a fine feline that lived nearby, they say he had been father to most of the fur kids around the area, and he might have even been my fur Dad, who knows. He had no special two-feet in his life. The funny thing with George was that he had cross-eyes, if you can picture that. Though he was, a beautiful fit Tiger striped chap, he was a bit wild, yet he had a peaceful gentle way and he was always smiling. He soon made friends with us all, so I

hoped he was my fur Dad. Kitz was his special fur best mate. They went everywhere together. The two of them used to chill out on the sun loungers together, sleeping & dreaming the hot sunny days away and out causing a stir in the neighbourhood every night. He was brave yet had a real relaxed way about him and really, I do not think anything scared George. He was what they called FEARLESS! All we fur girls would have liked George as a special friend, but we knew he only had eyes for Kitz. He did become a bit of a father figure to me. My Mom used to sit on the bench with George and give him funny tummy rubs; he was quite comfortable with the two-feet and I feel that he may well have liked to join our family. My last memory of George is when we left Spain in the early hours of the morning, and George came by to say "Adios", which is the Spanish word for "Goodbye". To this day, I do not know how he knew we were leaving, because even we were not sure what was happening then. However, his wildcat sense was always very strong. We were all four waiting inside our big travel box when he arrived, and poor Kitz was so frustrated and unable even to say goodbye to George. He tried to escape and bite his way out, but the box was made of strong stuff. George knew we were leaving and he must have known that he would never see us again. I think I even saw tears in his big sad cross-eyes. Our Mom gave him one last goodbye dinner, and I know she was very sad at that time too because I saw tears in her eyes. She wanted to take George with us, but Dad said that four fur babies were more than enough to take to ENG-land wherever that may be. We just hope that George can take care of himself and stay away from all the bad two-feet out there in Spain. Mom has promised Kitz that she will take a 'holiday' especially to check on George. Her two-feet friends have already checked on him, and apparently, he is still living wild, smiling, and still strong.

Vet Visits

We all hate going inside those tiny vet boxes. Each of us has our own personalised box kitted out with our names on the front, and all the mod kitty cons with a proper fleecy blanket and a drinking place and plenty of treats inside, but it is a frightening experience to be in that box totally trapped. It does have

small windows at the front, so we can see each other, but we make sure that Mom knows how much we hate it by wailing as loud as we can to try to make it stop. We make quite a tune. I think we should go into singing; we could be the first kitty band. Popcorn thinks she is already the star of 'X Factor', as she always gets on the picture box when that is on. I also practice my heavy breathing more at vet times, as I know that always worries my Mom more than anything does. I do genuinely have difficulty with my breathing, but sometimes it can be used to get what I want, for

instance when they are getting ready to go out and I don't want them to leave me I breathe a bit louder to try and keep Mom here by my side for longer. It never works out though, as she knows what I am up to. Now the vet is a very different matter, which I really do not like at all. We four in our boxes are taken into the Metal Beast one by one, and it is a wibbly, wobbly trip to get there as we are all getting too heavy for our Mom to carry these days. The Beast's growl is loud but our cries our louder. I am not sure why we need to go there as it is very stressful and then to make it worse, we wait for ages in our boxes. Our noses pressed up against the windows until the vet is ready to see us. I have no idea why they call it the vet but it is horrid. We take it in turns to go in. The vet is always a two-feet, sometimes a very nice feel one and other times not so nice. I think the most scared of us lot is me, because I am not too good with most of the two-feet. They always have this cold flat surface, onto which they pull each of us out of the box and try to tickle us and get friendly. I know what they are up to and I try to bite them and stretch out my claws to warn them off. The next thing they are jabbing sharp things into my body or they make my mouth open, or turn me over repeatedly. I sometimes stop and laugh when I imagine it happening to Purdy, because after all she is a Princess. It must be so humiliating for her Ha. Ha. The last time I was there, the vet actually put a new necklace on me. I think that is because I would not let my Mom put the necklace on me. I am not sure why we need to wear necklaces anyway. I knew what a necklace was already, as Tiger from my first life had mentioned them in many of his stories. He said that cats that live with two-feet have to wear them. It is strange that necklaces are not given to Princesses, and yet they wear crowns. Tiger had also mentioned this to me. Whenever we manage to get out of that vet house, it is such a relief, even though we have to get back into that box first and then be loaded into the Beast again for the ride home. We are happy because although we wail all the way home for effect, we know that we will not have to visit the vet again for quite a while. Well we hope so anyway!!!

When Purdy got sick

Purdy or 'The Poison Paw' as some of us renamed her was very vulnerable in the last bit of time when we
were living in Spain. We all thought that she was at the point of no
recovery and was heading towards The Rainbow Bridge. At that time Dad
had to spend a long time away from us, it was so long that I had almost
forgotten what he smelled like, but I did not really miss him. Because it
just meant I got more attention from Mom, however as Purdy is his
special Princess, she suffered the most from his absence. Purdy has never
been a big cat, but she started to get extremely small and frail and she
could not eat her food any more. Our Mom was very worried about her,
especially as Dad was away, and Mom felt responsible. At one time Purdy
was being sick after every meal and could not eat anything properly. We
all thought it was just fur-balls, but clearly, Purdy was in a lot of pain
and was crying a lot. Mom gave her special soft food and tried to give her
some real good stuff, even Milk! However, Purdy still hurt when she tried
to eat anything and she just got worse and worse. We did not know then
that we were shortly to be leaving Spain, and we all had dates for needle

pricks and other horrid stuff involving extra vet visits to make us ready for our big long journey.

On the day that Kitz was due to go to the vet for his needle prick, he ran away, so Mom took Purdy instead to replace Kitz. She looked so miserable in her carry box and even had to take off her crown to fit inside. Mom came home from the vet that day with an empty carry box, and we were all feeling sorry that we had called her bad names, because home did not seem the same without her royal smells around. Thankfully, it was not serious though. She only had her teeth cleaned at the vet and when Purdy got back home she took a little holiday, the two-feet pampered her, and we all made a real effort to be nicer to her; even Popcorn tried, but Purdy did not want our sympathy, she just sat in the deckchair all day with her crown by her side. I remember the days when Mom first encouraged Purdy to play with a ball. It was ever so funny and she looked so awkward trying to learn to play. She had never known about the idea of playing games before that, as I guess royalty are a bit serious and don't play around much, and I reckon she is still not convinced about it. I can relate to that idea though, as

my own life previously really had not involved any playing either. Maybe Princesses and we street cats have a lot in common. Purdy bullies Popcorn quite often and gets into big trouble with the two-feet because of it. I will not let her intimidate me and she knows not to even try. I just give her the look with my extra big eye and she backs right off. As for Kitz, he is quite a softie and Purdy can wrap him around her little paw. We think she might have had two-feet bonds before Dad rescued her, and maybe she had been left abandoned by them, as seems to happen to so many fur kids that we know over there in Spain. Anyway, Purdy survived her illness and since the big move from Spain and being reunited with Dad, she has completely recovered her appetite and actually has grown bigger. She did have another sick wobble recently but she only had a tooth removed and now the new vet has put her on a special medicine called Steroids to build her up, and she has turned into a real super cat. She is now quite big and strong and is always the first of us to eat at mealtimes. Purdy always makes a lot of noise to remind the two-feet that it is her time to eat. We all think it was being without her Daddy that made her sick. It is understandable, as every one of us deserves the love of special two-feet that transforms us from unwanted street cats, into 'real' home cats. We are the lucky ones, whilst some of our kind, remain unlucky and unloved until they reach The Rainbow Bridge alone.

Sweet and Sad Memories of the land of Lizards and Snakes

I think we would have stayed in Spain if Mom and Dad had been completely happy, but things changed a lot when Miss Lisa went over The Rainbow Bridge with Banff, and Dad got very sad. Spain had been my birthplace and I have both sweet and sad memories when I think of my time before my two-feet relationships. Yes, it was lonely often, but I was free and wild and did not need anybody, as I was a solitary soul, and I guess I was destined to be there at the time to learn my skills. It was a bit, like what

two-feet call school days I think. My days were full and mostly hot. We do not see any sign of that yellow hot ball in the sky now that we are in this ENG-land, (Mom calls it "Sunshine" and she misses it a lot!) it is mainly wet and cold here now. To be honest though, it could get too hot over there. When you have fur coats as we do, it is often difficult to stay cool enough, and with my breathing problems the hot, hot, hot, days could be a struggle and I slept lots under the shade of the trees, however as the sun cooled we did have some great fun out there chasing anything that moved. Now I feel I should explain something that you might find unpleasant, concerning the food chain of life and very important to understand. In the wild, every creature needs to hunt to survive, and that process does not start with a trip to Tesco's (Even though it does stock our favourite cat food). Each animal in the wild is at a different stage of that food chain, and we

39

are designed to be able to hunt those below us for our food that we need in the wild. Most of the two-feet do not really understand that we cats originated from the big cats; in fact, we are just like miniature Lions, Tigers, Pumas or Leopards who were invited into the homes of two-feet. They sometimes forget that it is our nature to hunt for our food; we also need to chew meat for our wellbeing, for example if we should purely eat the foods that the two-feet provide for us, we would not be able to remain healthy and our teeth may even fall out. (Just like Purdy) Kitz is well aware of this problem, so he has been providing raw food extras to help Purdy's mouth get well. I heard Mom and Dad talking about those moving treaty things one day, and found out that some of these things are called Lizards and Snakes and Frogs and Cicadas' I loved them all. The problem is when you played with them they only lasted a short while and then they stopped playing suddenly. Odd! The Lizards were weird as when you touched them they always threw away their tails, which were quite yummy if you like that kind of chewy taste, but I always prefer it when things are still moving really. Snakes were ok but they moved too fast, which I guess was quite good exercise for us fur faces. My favourite moving things were the Cicadas as they sung a good song and they jumped high until you took off their legs. Frogs jumped too, but they tasted horrid. Popcorn liked the Cicadas too and often we would both chase the same fellow until one of us took off a leg, which slowed him down, and then we got bored and moved on to a new game. (Please don't try any of this at home!). Kitz has always been a frog fan. They were usually too big to handle and he used to try to get his mouth around them, but it was a funny scene to watch him pulling faces, as we knew they always tasted so rank. As for Purdy, she did not hunt much. I am not sure her eyes are as good as they should be for a cat. She always tried to catch flying things like Butterflies, but most of the time she preferred to sleep her days away, and still does now. We all think she is a bit boring actually.

Since we have been here in the new place, which is a very long way from Spain, we have not seen any of those exciting things at all yet, it is strange because I have been looking for them every day and cannot find any of them around outside. I often wonder where they have gone.

Kitz has always been a bit of a favourite to all us fur girls; however, he really likes the two-feet best. Back then, we lived then by a lane that used to wind around and it ended up somewhere near George. I think that is how Kitz must have met George in the first place because every time the two-feet used to go past our place, Kitz would jump up and run by their side just like a dog would do until they went out of his territory. It was a dangerous thing to do, as you never knew if it was a good, or a bad two-feet at first, but Kitz is the most trusting cat that I have ever met. He likes to think that he is tough but he is a big softie at heart. Most of those two-feet who Kitz accompanied found him charming; and they usually laughed and petted him all the time. I know he was genuinely guiding them and making sure, they found their way along his own bit of road. Lucky there were not many Metal Beasts around there. We had a nice quiet spot really. Some hot nights we all used to roll around on our backs out there and those Beasts would growl and swerve out of our way. Another silly game we enjoyed to play was sitting on top of Mom and Dad's own Metal Beasts. It was good fun too. We used to wet our paws then we walked all over their roofs to make our marks. It was especially good fun to do that just after they had given their Metal Beast a wash and rub, then they found our little paw prints all over the top. We think it looked so pretty.

Passports and Journeys

I was ready to go before any of the others, my suitcase was packed and I would be sitting on top of it every day waiting for the big trip. I did not know exactly where or when or why we were going, but I was happy to go anywhere with my Mom. I knew we were leaving soon as Mom had bags full of stuff everywhere and she had been busy packing for a long time. In fact, our whole space was a bit upside down, and she had made us a special mini Cat-house to travel in. I wanted to make sure that I was not going to be left behind, so I continued to sit and sleep on the suitcase constantly, and sometimes I used to climb into that mini Cat-house to let her know that I was ok with it. I don't think the others realised that anything big was going to change, but change it certainly did! We all started going on lots of vet visits where the vet would be jabbing us many times and we were each given our own ID number and passport too. Mom told me that all these things were necessary for us to be able to stay together as a family, so I put up with it and did not mind too much really.

The day that we set off was quite strange, after we left home and watched George disappear in the distance we took off in the Metal Beast. Each of us had our suitcases and we were taken to the train station were we waited for the 'Kitty Express' to arrive 'Kitty' then took us into a big busy place called a city, and it was there that we had to wait for a really big Metal Beast to arrive which had all our stuff in it. Then all four of us cats got into the mini Cat-house inside. It was like a giant version of our vet boxes but they were all joined together so that we could be together, but each in a separate bit with tiny windows all around. I could see Purdy from where I was and I could hear Popcorn and Kitz upstairs. We

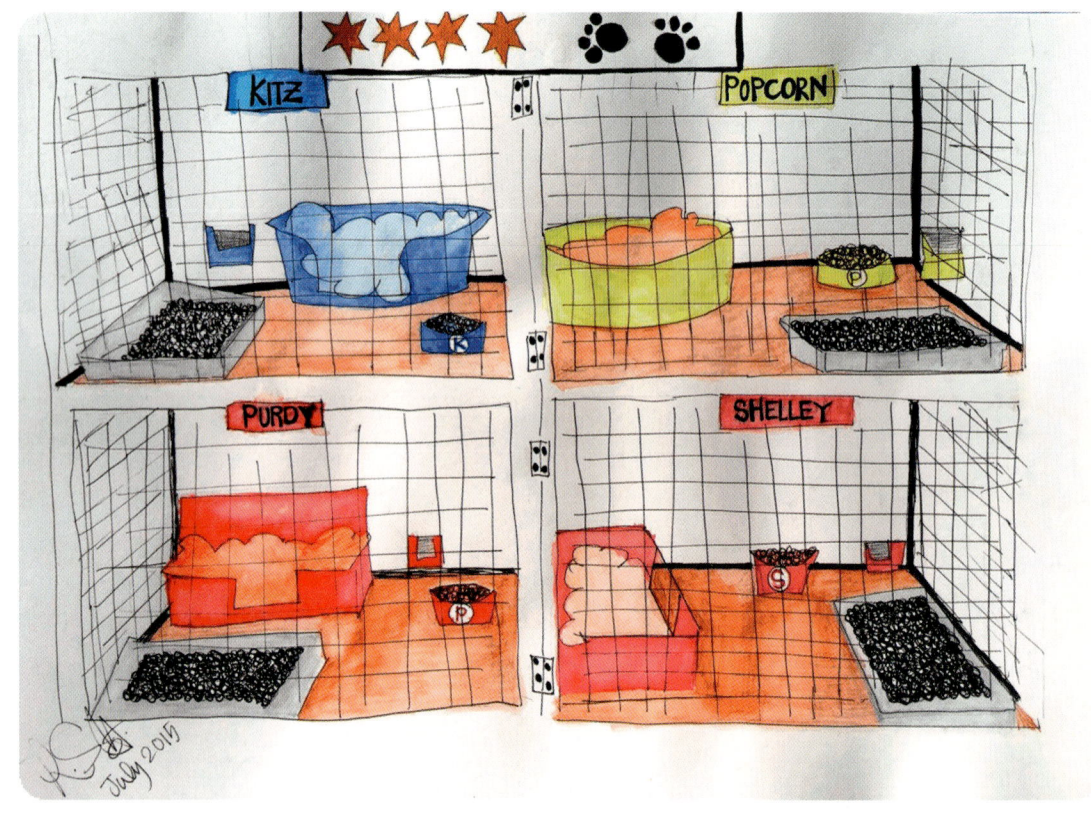

each had a bed and food and drink and a mini litter tray. Mom called it our four star accommodation. Probably because she had her four little stars safely inside. We were carried inside the belly of that extra large Metal Beast with all the rest of the stuff from the house. Tables, chairs, pictures, bags, surrounded us and Mom said we even had the kitchen sink in with us. However, I could not see that. I think Mom wanted us to feel comfortable. I slept for most of the journey because it was very dark in there and I just wanted to dream of what our new happy place would be like. The ride was very bumpy at times though and I made a bit of a mess of my space. So did Purdy. It did get a bit smelly in there. Every time the Beast opened its mouth, we got a chance to see a bit of the world outside and feel some cold air. It was really cold! Mom was inside the two-feet part of the Beast but she kept looking at us regularly to reassure us that we were almost there, although it seemed to take ages to get there. During the journey I just kept thinking of what a great time we had with our new friend 'Kitty Express' and I was looking forward to seeing her again as she promised to come and see us in our new home and take us on some great adventures. I will tell you more about those another time. When the Metal Beast stopped growling we were in a place called 'France' where Mom had to show our passports to some two-feet, also she waved a magic wand above us that told them who we were and what our special numbers were so that we did not have to speak to them. It was just as well, as they talked with different words that we had never heard before, but Mom seemed to understand them okay. It was scary because Mom could not find my special number with the magic wand at first and we were all worried that I might have been sent back to the beginning of the journey. Everything was fine, my number was found and we were all allowed onto the boat. It was very exciting as none of us had ever been to sea before, it was so much nicer than being inside any of the Metal Beasts and we swayed around in a way that sent us straight into a relaxing sleep. When we got to our destination it was extremely cold, but it was nice to see a familiar face, yes 'Kitty' our new friend was waiting at the other end to take us the last part of our journey to our new home where Daddy was waiting for us. Purdy and Mom were over the moon with happiness···

The Adventures of us in the Land of Eng

As you know the journey took us to ENG-land, and we had arrived. We were shivering, even Kitty was horrified, she said "Oh it's so cold here; you will have to make a fire to keep warm…" The home she took us to first was where Dad was waiting for us, it was not as bad as the Cat-house, as it did have a roof on

top, but it wasn't a friendly house and it smelled of cold and old water. Mom, and Dad both got sick, and my breathing got bad, and the others were very sad in that house. It was not exactly the dream that I had been dreaming on that long trip from Spain. Mom shouted at Dad all the time and told him that we can't stay here in this house, so Mom went looking for a new home for us all. The first day that we were allowed out into the big outside was a big shock for us. Dad had built us a huge cage, which was almost as tall as the house, but it was outside so that we could play and stay safe from all the Metal Beasts that growled loudly and moved quickly and constantly in front of the house. Even Popcorn could not get to the top of that cage; it was so high. She did try! Kitz used to sit on the top of an old log, which Dad had put there for us to scratch, and he would dream of our old world where he had been happy. At that house it was colder 'in' than 'out', even though it had a roof, so that was not a great start. I hope we never go back there! I will never forget the time we experienced the 'real' cold when the sky made a white thing called 'Snow'; We watched it come down fast from the sky, all white and beautiful, and when we went out to the cage to do our toilet that day our feet disappeared into that fluffy white cold stuff. It actually looked much nicer than it was, but it smelled so bad that our noses stopped working for a while. I thought mine was going to fall off, but luckily, it did not. The Princess Purdy and I often cuddled up real close with our tails curled around each other for comfort, also to keep warm. Even Mom and Dad used to cuddle right up close to us, so that our fur coats gave them extra warmth there; that bit was nice, but my dream had actually turned into a nightmare!

Our next home in ENG-land was the best...Our clever Mom found us a cat dream house!!! She calls it our cosy cottage in a hamlet with no big roads nearby, so we can be safe. It is quite interesting that in cat talk, the 'Eng' is a big animal that eats grass and makes a sound like this... "Moooo". Mom calls them 'Cows'., but we have always known them as 'Engs', and you did not often see them in Spain, so how strange it is that they call this place 'ENG-land' Odd really, because Engs are everywhere! At last we were free to roam, and roam we did. There was no need for a cage and it was an exciting outside space... I was the first (after Kitz) to do a tour of the area. I climbed walls, squeezed through hedges, stuck my head in holes, slid down roofs and sneaked through houses. One day I found some yummy smelling stuff on a table and after just one lick, I got a load of water flung at me from high. I have no idea where it came from, but I was soaked. It was a real mystery because when I got out of there I found no wet falling from the sky at all. If I were not so drenched, I would have thought I had dreamt it all. I discovered later that it had been the farmer's wife water bucket trick, whatever that is? It was not a very funny trick though; I think it is 'she' who owns the Engs. I have never returned to that place since. The others were also excited with their new freedom. Popcorn did a few trips out, but Kitz had already seen it all and got the cat necklace before any of us others. He had always been the great explorer. Speaking of which we all

(except Purdy) wear necklaces now, with coloured bells and barrels hanging from them, which we all dislike because it is so childish, but Mom says it keeps us safe, so whatever. Kitz keeps shaking off his bell. He is the master hunter and as such, he believes that he must remain bell free. Dad keeps putting new bells on his necklace every time he loses one, because he keeps bringing in small furry treats as gifts and Mom and Dad do not like it. I am not sure how that bell should stop him doing that, but it is a strange world. I have not yet found any small furry treats, only the big ENG ones and they scare me a bit. These large furry treats are the ones that make that odd sound of "MOOOOOO" and they flick their huge tails at me. One time it took me right off my feet. I think one day when I am bigger I will catch one and bring it back as a gift for Mom. How happy she would be! We all keep searching for the Lizards, Snakes and Cicadas, but so far have not found any here in the land of Eng. There are lots of flying things, which are everywhere, but so far, I have had no success with them either. I am concluding that my hunting days are almost over. Just one big ENG and then I may even consider retirement, like Purdy. We two can leave all that outdoor fun for the youngsters Kitz and Popcorn. Kitz is still being overfriendly with two-feet strangers. He talks to

Anybody! There was a two-feet in the garden today, he comes quite a lot and touches all the green stuff and things, but Kitz was following him around everywhere like a dog. Mom says it is the gardener. I think he is harmless enough, and by now I am sure he realises that it is we fur faces who run this place, and luckily he is not anything like that scary Marco the Midget Monster from before. Therefore, we are very happy at the cottage and we all want to stay here forever. I was thinking about things, and realised that since I met my Mom she has taken me already to five forever homes including the rest au rant. It is very tiring for a little cat that has to find new smells every time she moves home you know. Nevertheless, I am happy. We have already stayed at two places so far since we did that big journey from Spain, the place where we are now they call Cornwall, and it is very nice! Out is still mostly cold and wet, but where we are now inside it is warm and dry. Perhaps this is our 'forever forever' home! We can go out or stay inside whenever the sky is light, and then when the sky disappears we eat, and its bedtime. We all got used to our new routine nicely. Mom does not like us being outside when the sky leaves us, because of the foxes. I am not exactly sure what they are, but they sound interesting. Kitz is desperate to see this foxy thing, but Mom does not think it is a good idea. So far my favourite soft spots inside are the fluffy pink cushions that mom just got, obviously I love to be curled up on their big bed up at the top of the steps. You will always find Popcorn in many different spots, she is very unpredictable and prefers to be outside mostly with Kitz, but if she is inside she will usually be sleeping on top of the cooker, or sitting on one of the window ledges looking at the world, or in a box. Purdy is always on her throne next to the fire, and Kitz is everywhere.

New Treats and New Friends

I am very pleased with myself today. Just as Mom and Dad got home from work I actually found what I had been looking for, the sun had been shining all day and had brought out some tasty moving treats for us. I had half expected my first hunt in this new place to bring a furry thing, but this find was a long wriggly smooth thing with no fur; it would not keep still, which gave me great fun chasing it around. It was doing its little wriggly dance and I did get a good bite out of its tail and was intending to leave the rest for my Mom. It was so tasty, not like the big Snakes from before, this one was seriously lovely. It reminded me of the taste of Lizard from the old days. I made a bit of a mess, but managed to pull it in through the window and took it to my dinner dish; just as I was going to eat the rest my Dad picked it up, I think he was very pleased with my find as he took it away and looked at it for a very long time. I thought he had probably put it somewhere safe to eat later. I tried to find it. Dad did not even eat it, but he looked it up on 'Google' whatever that is, and discovered that what I had found was a 'slowworm', which is from the Lizard family. I rest my paw! Whilst we are on the subject of treats, as I explained earlier, for cats it is natural for us to hunt for pleasure. Our Mom does not really like it though, and sometimes she gets upset when she finds one of our furry or slimy gifts. Kitz keeps on finding mice with long noses. Today it really felt like being in our old hot world with the sunshine high in the sky, and our Mom was jolly, she was outside with us. At one point, we all watched as Kitz suddenly rushed into the bush and came out with a mouse in his mouth. Mom screamed at him to drop it, but he just kept growling to warn us all that it belonged to him, and he was determined to keep it. After a while of walking around with it sticking out of his mouth, it was headfirst with its little legs and tail wiggling around, and Mom was chasing him. Eventually Kitz put the mouse down on the grass and ate it. It has to be said that he is quite a good catch. I think he would have saved the juicy bits for our Mom, but she made it very clear that Mouse was not on her menu today. She did not even want the tail. Two-feet are very ungrateful. My hunting skills are okay (ish), but I have slowed down since I left the wild and came to

live with my family. I still do enjoy the fun of the chase, but when it comes to the crunch and it is time to eat it, I do not usually bother these days. It is probably because I never seem to feel hungry anymore, not like before when I was 'Ugly'; I like being beautiful 'Shelley' so much better! In fact since we have been living, here I am already good friends with a Hedgehog, Rabbit a Frog, a Squirrel, and I even met a Mouse and finally I saw a Fox yesterday and he was not scary at all. Being friends is so much nicer than hunting. We met some Gulls today, (huge birds) they were talking about The Rainbow Bridge and I remembered with sadness my friends and family that had gone there already. At first Kitz thought those Gulls might be nice tasty treats, and he started doing his "AKKA-KA-KA" bit, but the Gulls were thinking we could be their treats, so most of us got out of there quickly. (Remember what I said about the food chain). The Gulls are much too big for birds and their beaks look strong too. I am not ready for crossing any bridges just yet…, but Kitz did manage to get into a real scrape and he had a nasty encounter with one of those Gulls who mistook him for dinner. That Gull simply swooped down, took Kitz by the back of his neck, and lifted him high into the sky. When it let go of Kitz, there was a lot of damage and Mom found Kitz trying to hide with a pool of blood around him. Perhaps he has now learnt his lesson not to mess with creatures that are bigger than he is. The vet has given him some medicine and Dad has grounded him for a

few days rest. I met up with 'Kitty' this afternoon, and she promised to take us out again when Kitz is better. We have had many adventures with Kitty since our big trip here, but I shall save those stories for another day. Right now, I shall say "Goodnight and Sweet Dreams". It has been a long eventful day for a little cat, so I snuggle up on my Mom's fluffy pillow on their big soft bed, feeling safe and full of happiness. I am off to happy cat dreamland now because tomorrow is a new day, a new adventure, and because I am a cat.

Illustrations

- We cats do speak your language
- The AKKA-KA-KA sound
- My new sister
- Fond of looking at her reflection
- She wears a crown
- The Dude
- It says so on my Passport
- Am I ugly?
- We lived a tough life
- Our friends would be over the Rainbow Bridge by now
- It was really hard to stay alive
- Marco the Midget Monster
- Treats are for good cats only
- Mom wanted to be with Dad
- George
- Popcorn thinks she is already the star of X Factor
- Heading to the Rainbow Bridge
- She took a little Holiday
- Chasing anything that moved
- We would walk on top of the Metal Beasts with wet paws
- Someone's bitten off the top of my ear
- My suitcase was packed
- Four star accommodation
- ENG is a big creature that eats grass
- A huge cage which was almost as tall as the house
- New treats and new friends

Thank you for reading my book! Should you want to find out more about my family, my friends, and me you can join my face book group "Because I am a Cat", or check out my website: www.becauseiamacat.com where you will be able to give me feedback, also to keep updated on all the latest adventures and find the next books in this series....

...If Shelley's story "Because I am a cat" has made you want to welcome a cat into your life; remember first to check at your local animal rescue centres. There you will find many unwanted pets waiting for their forever homes. You will know exactly which cat to take home, as she/he will find you! You will have a friend for life. If you take good care of your cat, there will be nine lives in which to enjoy getting to know your best fur friend for many years ahead. Always be kind and gentle, always offer plenty of love, safety, routine, playtime, freedom, and allow her/him to be a cat!